ID0906416

ALIEN ABDUCTION

Anne Rooney

🌳 Crabtree Publishing Company

www.crabtreebooks.com

Crabtree Publishing Company
PMB 16A,
350 Fifth Avenue,
Suite 3308
New York, NY 10118

616 Welland Avenue,
St. Catharines, Ontario
L2M 5V6

Content development by
Shakespeare Squared

www.ShakespeareSquared.com

Published by Crabtree
Publishing Company © 2008

First published in Great Britain
in 2008 by ticktock Media Ltd,
2 Orchard Business Centre,
North Farm Road,
Tunbridge Wells, Kent, TN2 3XF

ticktock project editor:
Ruth Owen
ticktock project designer:
Sara Greasley
ticktock picture researcher:
Lizzie Knowles

With thanks to: Series Editors Honor Head
and Jean Coppendale

Picture credits (t=top; b=bottom; c=centre; l=left; r=right):
Baptism of Christ, c. 1710 (oil on canvas), Gelder, Aert de
(1645-1727)/ Fitzwilliam Museum, University of Cambridge,
UK./ The Bridgeman Art Library: 24. Bettmann/ Corbis: 15c,
21. Columbia/ Everett/ Rex Features: 29b. Corbis/
SuperStock: 6. ImageState: 1, 2, 4-5, 16-17, 19, 20. Jupiter
Images: 12-13. Uwe Krejci/ Getty Images: 28b. Charles &
Josette Lenars/ Corbis: 25l. Mary Evans Picture Library/
Alamy: 14c. NASA/ ESA/ H. Bond (STScl) and M. Barstow,
University of Leicester: 25r. Dale O'Dell/ Alamy: 7, 11.
Shutterstock: OFC, 5b, 8t, 8b, 9 all, 10, 14-15 background, 18,
20 (lady), 23. Michael Stone/ Alamy: 22c. Darren Winter/
Corbis: 28t. L. Zacharie/ Alamy: 26-27.

Every effort has been made to trace copyright holders, and we
apologize in advance for any omissions. We would be pleased to
insert the appropriate acknowledgments in any subsequent
edition of this publication.

Library and Archives Canada Cataloguing in Publication

Rooney, Anne
    Alien abduction / Anne Rooney.

(Crabtree contact)
Includes index.
ISBN 978-0-7787-3762-9 (bound).
--ISBN 978-0-7787-3784-1 (pbk.)

        1. Alien abduction--Juvenile literature. 2. Human-alien
encounters--Juvenile literature. I. Title. II. Series.

BF2050.R66 2008   j001.942   C2008-901171-6

Library of Congress Cataloging-in-Publication Data

Rooney, Anne.
    Alien abduction / Anne Rooney.
        p. cm. -- (Crabtree contact)
    Includes index.
    ISBN-13: 978-0-7787-3784-1 (pbk. : alk. paper)
    ISBN-10: 0-7787-3784-5 (pbk. : alk. paper)
    ISBN-13: 978-0-7787-3762-9 (reinforced library binding : alk. paper)
    ISBN-10: 0-7787-3762-4 (reinforced library binding : alk. paper)
    1. Alien abduction--Juvenile literature. 2. Human-alien
encounters--Juvenile literature. I. Title. II. Series.

    BF2050.R66 2008
    001.942--dc22

                                                            2008006153

CONTENTS

WATCH OUT, ALIENS ABOUT!

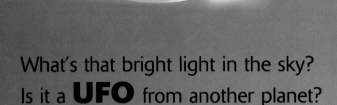

What's that bright light in the sky?
Is it a **UFO** from another planet?

Thousands of people say they have seen a UFO.
Many people say they have had contact with aliens.

Some people believe they have been **abducted** by aliens.

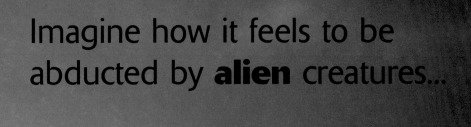

Imagine how it feels to be abducted by **alien** creatures...

ALIEN ALERT!

A **survey** in the United States found that 1 in 50 people believe they may have been abducted by aliens.

ABDUCTION

Imagine...

...you wake in the night.

A bright white light is shining in the window. A gray alien with bulging eyes is watching you.

You can't move!

A beam of light carries you out of the window and into the alien's spacecraft.

You are helpless!

ON THE SPACECRAFT

You wake up in a strange room.
You are strapped to a table.

Aliens examine your body.
They prod and poke you.

They take some of
your blood.

An alien pulls out
your eyeball.

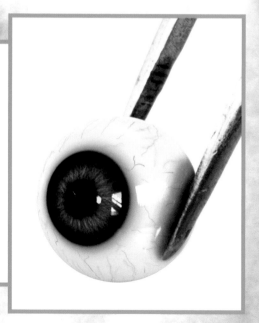

Implant

The alien puts an **implant** in the hole and then puts your eyeball back.

Some people believe implants send radio signals back to the aliens. This might help the aliens track their **abductees** and find them again.

FLASHBACKS

You wake up in your bed,
but you remember nothing.

You have painful **scars** and strange
burns that you don't remember getting.

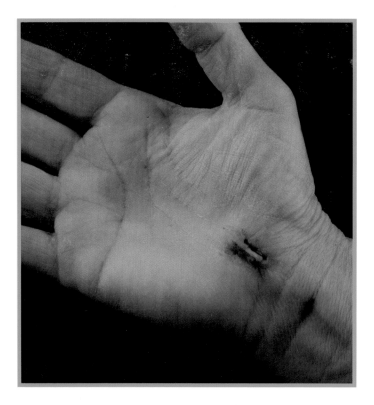

You feel scared and you feel ill.
You have **flashbacks** during the
day and strange dreams at night.
Weeks pass, and slowly you
remember.

To your horror, you realize you
have been abducted by aliens.

You tell other people.

Many laugh, but some people recognize your story. You have all been abducted by aliens.

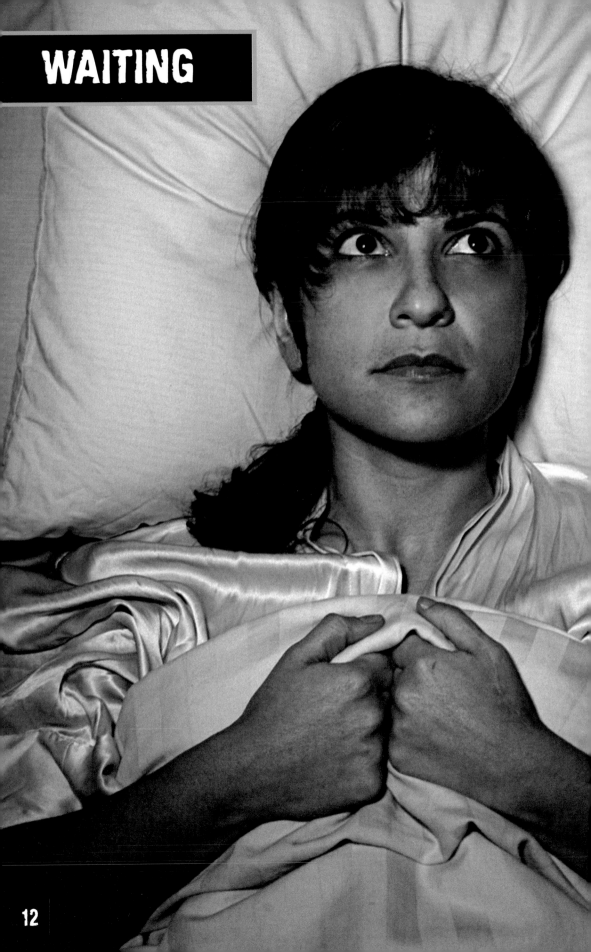

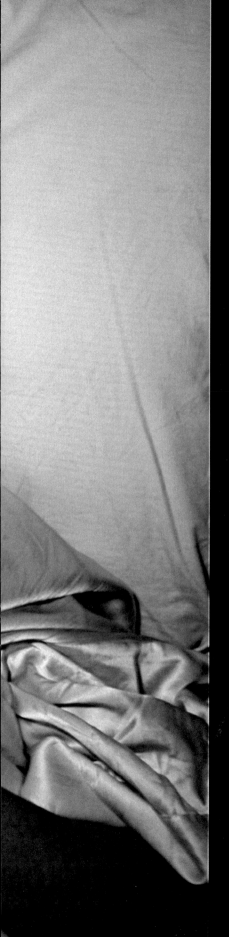

Every night you wait, terrified
you might be taken again.

Each morning you look for new
marks on your body.

All you can think is — what will
they do to me next?

Will they
hurt me again?

It's terrifying to imagine, isn't it?

But many people say this has really
happened to them!

BETTY AND BARNEY HILL

In September 1961, Betty and Barney Hill from New Hampshire were chased by a spaceship.

They tried to escape but they were abducted from their car.

At first Betty and Barney didn't remember what happened. But they had **strange marks** on their bodies. They also lost two hours of time.

Later, Betty had **terrifying dreams.** She started to remember.

Betty remembered being taken to a spaceship by short aliens. They had large heads and eyes.

The aliens examined Betty and Barney.

Betty and Barney drew a picture of the spaceship. Betty also drew a map the aliens showed her of their home **star system**.

ALIEN EYES

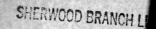

"I felt like the eyes had pushed into my eyes. All I see are these eyes."

Abductee, Barney Hill

TRAVIS WALTON

One evening in 1975, seven men saw a UFO.

The men were working in a forest. As they drove home, they saw a strange light.

One of the men, named Travis Walton, went to investigate.

Travis was **paralyzed** by a beam of light from a UFO.
His friends thought he was dead! They drove away.

When the men returned, Travis was gone.

Five days later, Travis turned up in a nearby town.
He said he had been abducted and examined by aliens.

Description of the Travis Walton aliens

Large, bald head

No eyelashes or eyebrows

White, marshmallow-looking skin

Mouths that didn't move

No fingernails

Just under 5 feet (1.5 meters) tall

FACT OR FICTION?

Usually no one sees an abduction.
This makes it hard to know if it's real.

Linda Napolitano from New York believed
she had been abducted many times.

In 1989, many people saw Linda being abducted.

They watched as she floated from her apartment
building toward a spaceship!

Sometimes abductees draw pictures of aliens.

The pictures often look the same as pictures drawn by other abductees.

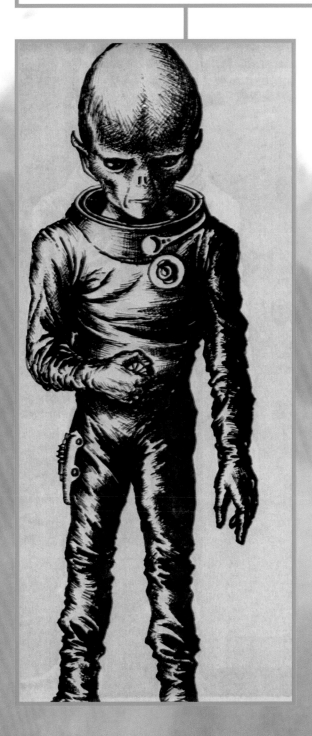

But, the pictures also look like aliens in movies.

Are these people remembering aliens that they have seen in movies?

This drawing was made from descriptions given by about 300 people who had seen aliens. All the people remembered the same details.

Some people think aliens have watched us for thousands of years.

These cave paintings are from Australia. They are more than 10,000 years old!

In the Nazca Desert in Peru there are giant pictures on the ground.
The pictures are known as the **Nazca Lines**.
Some of the pictures are more than 2,000 years old.
They can only be seen from a plane.

This picture is known as *The Spaceman*.

No one knows for sure why the pictures were made.

ALIENS FROM HISTORY 2

This painting was painted in 1710.

The painting is called *Baptism of Christ*. It was painted by Dutch artist Aert de Gelder.

Does it show a beam of light from a UFO?

The Dogon people live in Mali in West Africa.
They tell stories of visitors from the three Sirius stars.

The stories have been told for many years.
But one star wasn't discovered by scientists until 1999.

A Dogon ceremony

Sirius A is the biggest star. Sirius B is the tiny light spot in the bottom left of the above picture. Sirius C can't be seen — it is only visible through radio **telescopes**.

How can the Dogon know about Sirius C, the third star?

Did aliens tell the Dogon about the third star long ago?

OUR TURN

There is a story that a UFO crashed in Roswell, New Mexico in 1947.

Many people believe that dead alien bodies were found at the crash site.

The bodies were taken to a secret US Air Force base.

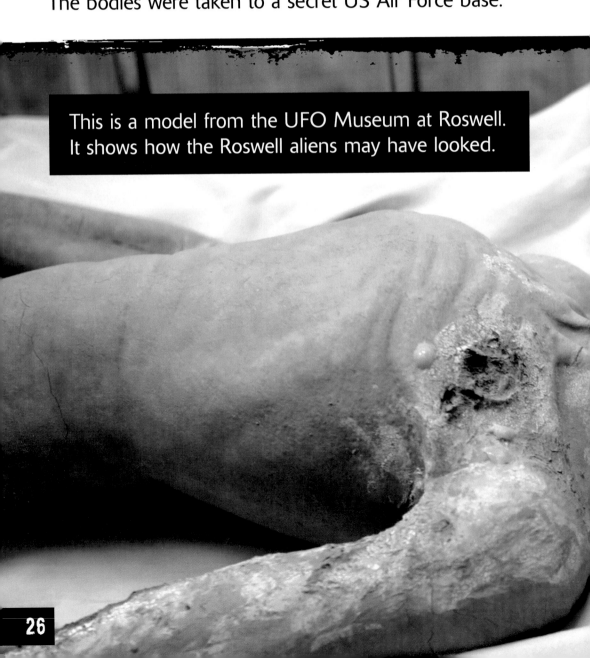

This is a model from the UFO Museum at Roswell. It shows how the Roswell aliens may have looked.

In 1995, a video tape was shown to the world.
It showed a **dead alien** being examined!

The video tape turned out to be **fake**.

But many people believe the Roswell story is true.
They believe that somewhere there are real alien bodies.

They are hidden in a **top secret** place
where they are examined by scientists.

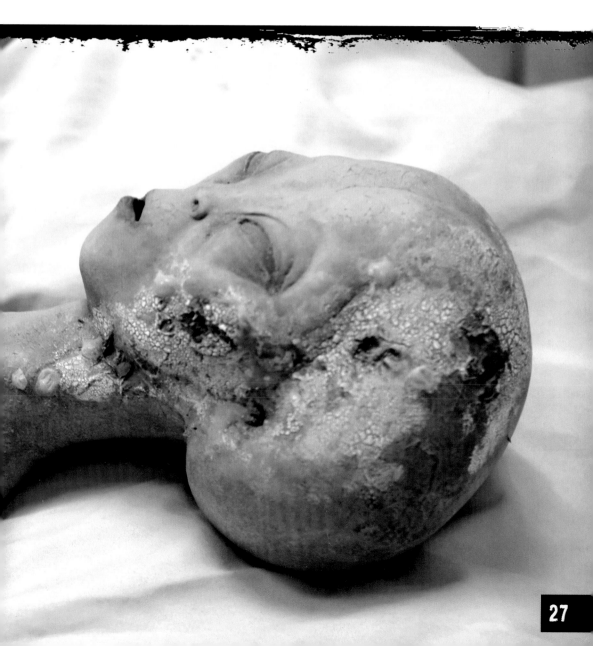

ALIEN SPOTTER'S GUIDE

Most people who are abducted by aliens say they were taken by Alien Grays. But some people say they have seen other types of aliens.

ALIEN GRAYS

- Large eyes
- Bald
- Gray skin
- 3 to 5 feet (0.9-1.5 meters) tall

NORDIC ALIENS

- Blond or white hair
- Blue eyes
- Pale skin
- Very strong
- 6 to 7 feet (1.8-2.1 meters) tall

- Claws
- Scaly skin
- Long tongue
- 5 to 8 feet (1.5-2.4 meters) tall

Some people who report seeing aliens say they are visited by men in black.
They tell them not to talk about what they saw.

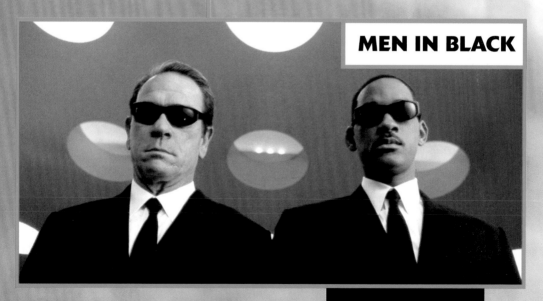

MEN IN BLACK

Some people think the men in black might be government agents. Others believe the men in black are aliens in disguise.

- Eyes hidden
- Black suits

NEED-TO-KNOW WORDS

abducted To be kidnapped

abductee A person who has been abducted, or kidnapped

alien A living being who is not from planet Earth

fake Something that is not real

flashback A sudden very clear memory of something that has happened in the past

implant A small piece of equipment put in a person's body by aliens. Some people believe implants send radio signals to aliens. This might help the aliens find the person in the future to abduct them again.

Nazca Lines Huge pictures in the Nazca Desert in Peru. The lines of the pictures were made by picking up stones to uncover the ground underneath which is a different color.

Nordic People who come from Northern Europe — they are usually tall and blond

paralyzed Unable to move

reptilian A creature that looks like a reptile — for example, it has scaly skin. Snakes and lizards are reptiles.

scars Marks left on the skin where a wound has healed

star system A small number of stars which travel around each other

survey A set of questions to ask people to collect information

telescope A tool for looking at things which are far away. A telescope may pick up light or radio waves.

UFO An Unidentified Flying Object. Many people believe that lights and objects in the sky which cannot be identified are alien spacecraft.

CLOSE ENCOUNTERS

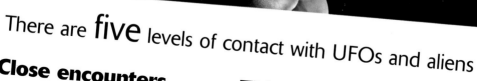

There are **five** levels of contact with UFOs and aliens

- **Close encounters of the first kind**
  Seeing a UFO within 300 feet (91 meters) or so

- **Second kind**
  Finding signs of a UFO, such as a crashed spacecraft

- **Third kind**
  Seeing aliens near a UFO

- **Fourth kind**
  Being abducted by aliens

- **Fifth kind**
  Meeting with aliens or making contact with a UFO

ALIENS ONLINE

Websites

http://www.seti.org/
The website of SETI (Search for Extraterrestrial Intelligence)

http://www.ufoevidence.org/photographs/view/featuredphotos.htm
This website features hundreds of photographs of UFOs

http://www.roswellufomuseum.com/incident.htm
A report on the Roswell crash from the UFO museum at Roswell

Publisher's note to educators and parents:
Our editors have carefully reviewed these websites to ensure that they are suitable for children. Many websites change frequently, however, and we cannot guarantee that a site's future contents will continue to meet our high standards of quality and educational value. Be advised that children should be closely supervised whenever they access the Internet.

INDEX

Printed in the U.S.A